CAMBRIDGE PRIMARY
Science

Learner's Book

2

Jon Board and Alan Cross

CAMBRIDGE
UNIVERSITY PRESS

CAMBRIDGE
UNIVERSITY PRESS

University Printing House, Cambridge CB2 8BS, United Kingdom

Cambridge University Press is part of the University of Cambridge.

It furthers the University's mission by disseminating knowledge in the pursuit of education, learning and research at the highest international levels of excellence.

Information on this title: education.cambridge.org

First published 2014
5th printing 2015

Printed in the United Kingdom by Latimer Trend

Cover artwork: Bill Bolton

A catalogue record for this publication is available from the British Library

ISBN 978-1-107-61139-9 Paperback

....

NOTICE TO TEACHERS
References to Activities contained in these resources are provided 'as is' and information provided is on the understanding that teachers and technicians shall undertake a thorough and appropriate risk assessment before undertaking any of the Activities listed. Cambridge University Press makes no warranties, representations or claims of any kind concerning the Activities. To the extent permitted by law, Cambridge University Press will not be liable for any loss, injury, claim, liability or damage of any kind resulting from the use of the Activities.

Introduction

The *Cambridge Primary Science* series has been developed to match the Cambridge International Examinations Primary Science curriculum framework. It is a fun, flexible and easy-to-use course that gives both learners and teachers the support they need. In keeping with the aims of the curriculum itself, it encourages learners to actively engage with the content, and develop enquiry skills as well as subject knowledge.

This Learner's Book for Stage 2 covers all the content from Stage 2 of the curriculum framework. The topics are covered in the order in which they are presented in the curriculum for easy navigation. But they can be taught in any order that is most appropriate to you.

The content pages contain many images and questions that you can use as a basis for class discussions. The emphasis in this stage is on linking what learners know about everyday life to scientific ideas.

Throughout the book, you will find ideas for practical activities which will help learners to develop their Scientific Enquiry skills as well as introduce them to the thrill of scientific discovery.

'Check your progress' questions at the end of each unit can be used to assess learners' understanding.

We strongly advise you to use the Teacher's Resource for Stage 2, ISBN 978-1-107-61148-1, alongside this book. This resource contains extensive guidance on all the topics, ideas for classroom activities, and guidance notes on all the activities presented in this Learner's Book. You will also find a large collection of worksheets, and answers to all the questions from the Stage 2 products.

Also available is the Activity Book for Stage 2, ISBN 978-1-107-61143-6. This book offers a variety of exercises to help learners consolidate understanding, practise vocabulary, apply knowledge to new situations and develop enquiry skills. Learners can complete the exercises in class or be given them as homework.

We hope you enjoy using this series.

With best wishes,
The Cambridge Primary Science team

Contents

Going outside

1.1 Different places to live

What do animals and plants need to live?

Look at the pictures. Which animals and plants live in each environment? What differences can you see?

Activity 1.1

Compare two different places

Go outside. Look for two places that are **different**, like a wet place and a dry place.

Measure the two places. Make sure they are the same size.

What can you find? Can you find any **minibeasts**?

Record the animals and plants you find in each place. Compare them.

What have you found out?

You will need:

a clipboard
a stopwatch or watch
something to measure with • a digital camera

This place is sunny.

It's shady over there.

What animals and plants live in these environments?

What you have learnt

◉ Environments can be different or similar.

◉ Different plants and animals live in different environments.

1.2 Can we care for our environment?

This beach is covered with **litter**. **Sewage** is flowing into the sea.

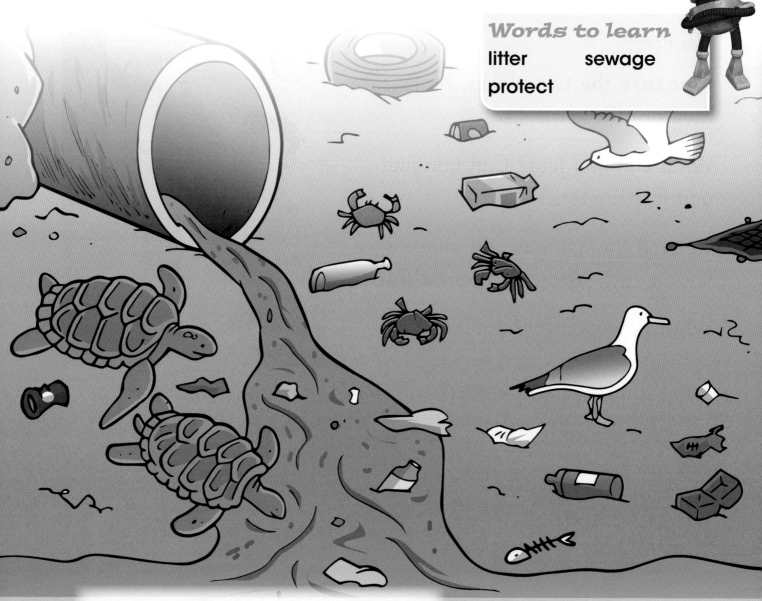

Words to learn
litter   sewage
protect

Do you think litter and sewage can harm the wildlife near the beach?

What can we do to help **protect** the wildlife?

Activity 1.2

Our environment

You will need:

a clipboard
a digital camera

Go outside and look around. Can you see places where people do not look after the environment?

Write, draw or photograph what you see.

How could people look after the environment better?

What could you do to help? Talk about your ideas.

Environmental groups are groups of people who help to look after the environment.

What you have learnt

🌀 You can look after your environment in different ways.

1.3 Our weather

Each day the **temperature**, **wind** and amount of Sun and **rain** can change. This is our **weather**.

The weather makes us think about what we do and what we wear.

Look at the pictures.

Why are the children wearing these clothes?

Activity 1.3

Today's weather

You will need:

large poster paper
a digital camera

Talk about the weather today.
Is it the **same** as yesterday?

Is it **sunny** or **cloudy**?

Is it **warm** or **cold**? Is it **frosty**?

Is there any rain, **snow** or **hail**?

How windy is it?

Make a poster to show what the weather is like.

The weather is not always the same.

Look at the picture. You can see a rainbow when it rains and the Sun is shining at the same time.

What you have learnt

🌀 You can look at the weather and draw or write down what you see.

1.4 Extreme weather

Have you ever seen the **extreme** weather in these pictures?

How would you keep safe in this weather?

Weather **forecasters** are scientists who tell us what the weather will be like. Satellites in space look down at the **Earth** and collect information. They help us forecast what weather will happen.

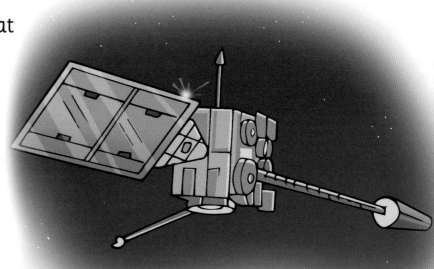

Look at the picture. There is a very bad storm under these clouds.

The **storm** is moving nearer the land.

What will happen to the weather on the land?

Activity 1.4

Keeping safe in extreme weather

Look at books or the internet.

You will need:

large poster paper
access to the internet

Do some **research** about one type of extreme weather. You could choose weather like heavy snow, hurricanes or tornados.

Make a poster to show what to wear and how to keep safe in this weather.

What you have learnt

There are different types of extreme weather.

1.5 Check your progress

1

dry place   wet place

eagle   frog   duck   goat   lion   fish

    a Which animals might live in the dry place?

    b Which animals might live in the wet place?

2 Some learners compared the number of plants and minibeasts found in two different places in their school. This is what they found.

Place	Number of minibeasts found	Number of plants found
A	15	25
B	5	3

    a Which place is best for minibeasts and plants to live in?

    b Why do you think this place is better for minibeasts and plants to live in?

3 What could we do to solve the problems in these environments?

A

B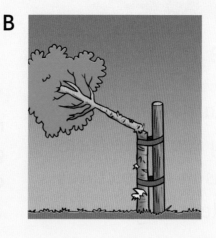

C

4 Some learners measured the amount of rain each day and drew this block graph.

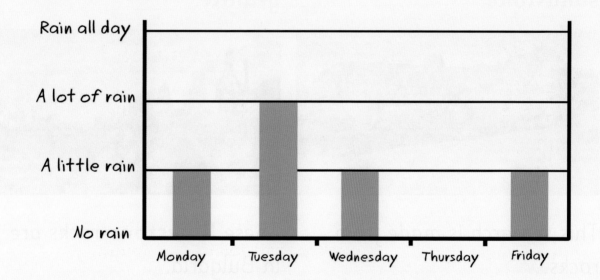

a On how many days did it rain?

b On which day was there most rain?

c On which day was there no rain?

d How much rain might there be on Saturday?

2 Looking at rocks

2.1 What are rocks?

The surface of the Earth is made of **rock**. You can easily see some rocks above the ground, as in the pictures. Others are deep under the ground or under water.

This rock is made of **sandstone**.

These rocks are made of **granite**.

This sea arch is made from rocks.

These **limestone** rocks are in Bulgaria.

There are many different types of rock. They have different colours. They can be hard or soft. They can be small or large.

A **quarry** is a place where rocks are dug from the ground. The rocks are taken from the quarry for us to use. Workers use machines to dig and move the rocks.

Activity 2.1

Comparing rocks

Collect some different rock samples. Look carefully at each of them.

Can you see any differences?

Draw what you see.

What you have learnt

🌀 Rocks cover the Earth's surface.

🌀 Some rocks are found under the ground.

🌀 There are different types of rocks.

2.2 Uses of rocks

Different rocks are used for different jobs. We use rocks to build roads, walls, houses and to make other things.

Diamond is very hard. It is used in jewellery and also in cutting machines.

Granite is very strong. It is often used in buildings.

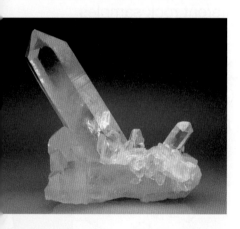

Quartz rocks are found all over the Earth. Clocks and radios use quartz.

Slate is hard and smooth. It is used for floor and roof tiles.

Marble is a hard, strong and smooth rock. It is used in many types of decoration and building.

Activity 2.2

Using rocks

Look around your school for rocks that have been used to make paths, walls, floors and roads.

You will need:

a hand lens

Look at the rocks carefully.

Can you see patterns? What colour are the rocks?

Why was that rock used?

Write down or draw what you find out.

What you have learnt

🌀 Different rocks are used for different things.

2.3 Soil

Rocks can be found in **soil**.

We use soil to grow our food. Without soil we would have no food.

Look at some soil. You will see:

- living things

- things that have died

- small pieces of rock.

Soil needs all these things.

Large rocks under the soil wear down slowly. They break into smaller pieces. The smaller pieces end up in the soil.

These small rocks can make the soil **sandy** (like **sand**) or more like **clay**.

Sometimes a rock in soil is called a **stone**.

Activity 2.3

Finding the rock in soil

Look at each soil sample. Do they look the same?

Put a little of each soil into its own bowl of water.

Shake the bowl slowly so that the water moves around the bowl.

Look at the pieces of rock and other material.

Draw what you see in the soil.

Say how the soils are different.

What you have learnt

🌀 Soil has rocks in it.

2.4 Other natural materials

Rocks are **natural** materials. They come from the ground.

Natural materials come from nature.

There are many other natural materials, like rubber. Rubber comes from a tree.

What natural materials can you see in the picture?

Here are some other natural materials.

cotton

wood

slate

plastic

paper

glass

These materials are **man-made**. They are made by people.

Activity 2.4

Finding materials

Walk around your school. Look for different materials.

Talk about the materials you find.

Are they natural or are they man-made?

Where did each material come from?

Draw the material and where it came from.

What you have learnt

🌀 Some materials are natural and some materials are man-made.

2.5 Check your progress

1 Can you name the rocks A, B, C and D?

Granite: very hard, with small pieces of many colours

Marble: hard, smooth, white, but can have other colours

Limestone: grey, can be scratched with steel, can contain fossils

Sandstone: red, brown or orange, can be scratched with steel, grains of sand can be scratched off

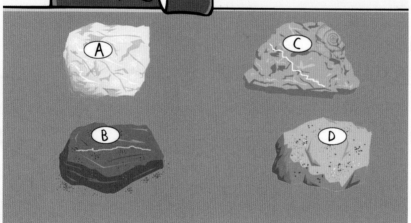

2 Which one of these is not made of rock?

a a mountain

b the surface of the Earth

c a river

d the sea floor

3 This building has columns made of marble. Why do we use marble for building things?

4 Why does soil have pieces of rock in it?

5 What natural material is used to make each of the things shown below?

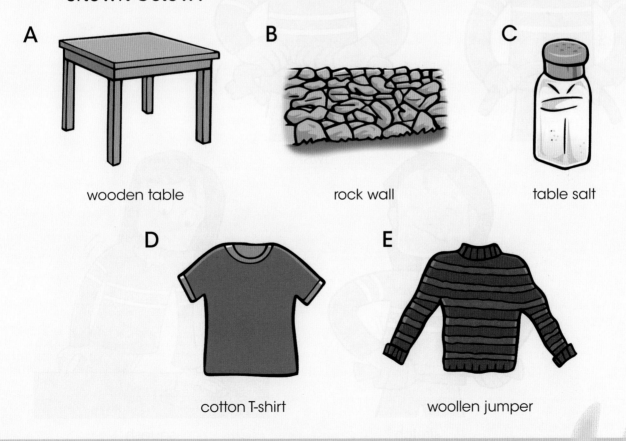

A wooden table

B rock wall

C table salt

D cotton T-shirt

E woollen jumper

3 Changing materials

3.1 Materials changing shape

You can **bend**, **twist**, **stretch**, and **squash** most materials. This will **change** the **shape** of the materials.

Words to learn

bend	twist
stretch	squash
change	shape

bend

twist

stretch

squash

Activity 2.1

Squashing

Which materials do you think will change shape when they are squashed?

Draw the materials before you squash them.

Press each one with your finger.

Talk to your friends. How does the shape change? Does the material keep its new shape when you take your finger away?

Draw each material after you have squashed it.

We use materials which squash and stretch to make us comfortable.

Other materials do not change shape so easily. We use these materials to make things which must be strong.

What you have learnt

🌀 We can change the shape of some materials by bending, twisting, stretching and squashing.

3.2 Bending and twisting

We can bend some materials using our hands. Examples are **dough** and modelling clay.

Word to learn
dough

We can bend other materials by using heat and tools.

This screen was made by heating metal and then bending it using tools.

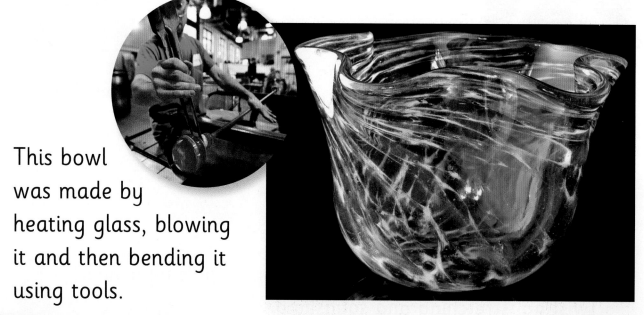

This bowl was made by heating glass, blowing it and then bending it using tools.

These materials have been twisted.

Which do you think you can twist with your hands?

Activity 3.2

Bending and twisting dough

Take a lump of dough.

Bend it and twist it to make an interesting shape.

Make some more shapes.

Draw the shapes you make.

What you have learnt

🌀 We can change the shape of materials by bending and twisting them.

3.3 Fantastic elastic

What material is the rope made from?

The rope tied to the bungee jumper is made from a material that will stretch.

Materials that will stretch are called **elastic** materials.

Rubber is a natural elastic material. It is made from the sap of the rubber tree.

Activity 3.3

Looking at elastic bands

Try to answer this question: which elastic band stretches the most?

Look at the pictures to see what to do.

What could go wrong in the pictures? How could you get hurt?

How will you tell others what you find out?

Sports players use elastic materials to train their muscles.

What you have learnt

🌀 Elastic materials change when they are stretched.

3.4 Heating and cooling

Words to learn

heat   hot
melt   cool
liquid   solid
ice

Pancake Recipe

Can you find ten different materials in this picture?

Which materials are being changed by **heat**?

Activity 3.4

Warming foods

You will need:

different foods
cling film or metal foil
a stopwatch

Wrap up a piece of chocolate. Hold it in your hand for two minutes.

What do you notice?

Does it make a difference if you hold it for longer?

Try this with other foods.

Compare what happens with the foods. Is there a pattern?

When a candle burns, the **hot** flame begins to **melt** the wax.

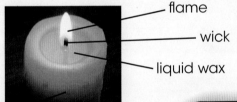

flame

wick

liquid wax

solid wax

You can also **cool** materials. A **liquid** will change to a **solid** if it is cooled to a low enough temperature. If water is put into a freezer it changes to **ice**.

What you have learnt

🌀 Some materials change when they are heated or cooled.

3.5 Why is the sea salty?

The sea is salty. Where does the salt come from?

Salt comes from rocks on land. Rivers and rain wash the salt into the sea.

Salt comes from rocks at the bottom of the sea.

People can get salt from the sea and from rocks under the ground.

The hot Sun is used to dry up pools of seawater. The salt is left behind.

Salt is dug from rocks under the ground.

Activity 3.5

Dissolving materials in water

What do you think will happen when Tara pours salt into the water?

Try it. Stir the water. What do you see?

You will need:

salt • water
a beaker • a spoon
other materials to test

We say the salt **dissolves**.

Can you dissolve more salt into the water?

Now try to dissolve some other materials. First **predict** which ones will dissolve and which will not.

How will you measure the amount of material you add to make sure the test is **fair**?

Tell others what happened.

What you have learnt

🌀 Some materials dissolve in water.

3.6 Check your progress

1 Carlo the clown has finished his show.

Can you answer these questions?

a How has the balloon in Carlo's hand changed shape?

b Carlo has dropped the plates. What has happened to the shape of some plates?

c Carlo has crashed his car. What has happened to the shape of the car?

2 Juno used different elastic bands to flick three identical paper aeroplanes.

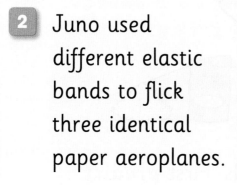

Elastic	Distance paper plane flew in metres
very thin elastic	2
thin elastic	4
thick elastic	6

a Which elastic made the plane fly furthest?

b Which elastic made the plane fly the shortest distance?

c What would happen if Juno used string instead of elastic?

3 What happens to these materials when they are heated?

   a chocolate   b butter   c ice

4 What happens to these materials when they are put in a freezer?

   a water

   b cooking oil

   c warm liquid chocolate

5 Musa stirred sugar into cups of warm water.

In cup a he could dissolve 2 spoonfuls.
In cup b he could dissolve 4 spoonfuls.
In cup c he could dissolve 7 spoonfuls.

If he tried this with sand instead of sugar, what would happen?

4 Light and dark

4.1 Light sources

A light source makes **light**.

How many light sources can you see here?

Words to learn

light   reflect

Moon   Sun

These objects are **not** light sources. They do not make light.

Some objects reflect light. The light bounces off them.

The Moon reflects light from the Sun. Water and mirrors reflect light.

Activity 4.1

Is it a light source?

Take some objects into a dark place.

Can you predict which objects are light sources?

Objects that are not light sources will look dark.

What you have learnt

- Light sources make light.
- The Sun is a light source.
- There are many other light sources.

4.2 Darkness

Hafeez is in his bedroom.

It is quite **dark** in his bedroom but there is some light.

Can you see how light is getting in?

I can see in the dark!

When there is very little or no light, we say it is dark. We need some light to see.

It is dark in this cave. The man has a **torch**. The torch makes light so he can see.

Activity 4.2

Can you see in the dark?

Kiri wants to see what is in the box, but it is dark. She cannot see anything.

Kiri is using a torch. Now there is light in the box. She can see inside.

Can you see in the dark?

Try looking into a dark box yourself to find out.

What you have learnt

- Darkness is when there is very little or no light.
- We cannot see without some light.

4.3 Making shadows

A **shadow** is made when an object blocks light.

Activity 4.3

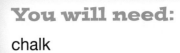

Making shadows in the Sun

Emeka is blocking the light. His shadow is dark because there is less light.

Umar is drawing around the shadow with chalk.

Try this outside. Look carefully at the shadow. Draw what you see.

Mia has two shadows. Can you see why?

What you have learnt

🌀 Shadows happen when objects block light.

🌀 The shadow is dark because there is less light there.

4.4 Shadow shapes

Shadows do not always look like the object that makes them.

Shadows can be a different shape.

Shadows have no colour. They are always dark.

Shadows have no details like eyes or a mouth.

Activity 4.4a

Making animal shadows

Try making these shadow animals with your hands.

Activity 4.4b

Making shadow puppets

Sara and Nasreen are making shadow puppets.

Try making your own shadow puppets.

Tell others how the shadow is made.

You will need:

card · scissors
glue · a light source
a screen

What you have learnt

🌀 Shadows can look different to the objects that make them.

🌀 Shadows have no details. They are always dark.

1 Which of these are light sources?

A   B   C

D   E

2 Drisha has lost her ball.

a Why can't she find it?

b What could she use to help her to find the ball?

3 What is wrong with these shadows?

4 Lucas has made a puppet. How can he make a shadow with his puppet?

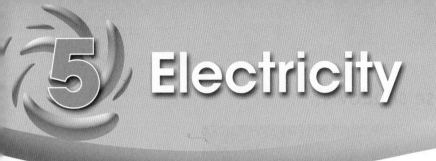

5 Electricity

5.1 Electricity around us

Electricity is all around us.
We can use it to make light or sound.
We can use it to heat things up or
cool things down.
We can use it to make things move.

Look at the picture. Which things use electricity?

Things that you plug in use **mains electricity**. Mains electricity is very powerful. It is made in power stations like this one. Can you see the wires?

A **cell** can store electricity. A cell is often called a **battery**. Cells are used for things that people carry like torches or mobile phones.

There are different kinds of cells.

Activity 5.1

Electricity around us

Look around your school. Which things use electricity?

Draw some things that use cells and some things that use mains electricity.

What you have learnt

- Electricity is very useful.
- Electricity comes from the mains or from cells.

5.2 Staying safe

Electricity moves in the metal part of a **wire**. The metal should be covered with plastic.

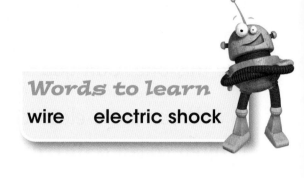

This wire is damaged.

Anyone touching the metal would get an **electric shock** and could die. Never use a damaged wire.

Never put anything into the holes of a wall socket. The metal parts inside could give you an electric shock.

Mains electricity can move through water. Never touch anything that uses mains electricity with wet hands.

Never use mains electricity near water.

Activity 5.2

Electrical safety

Make a poster that shows others how to stay safe with electricity.

What you have learnt

- 🌀 Take care when using electricity.
- 🌀 Mains electricity can be dangerous.
- 🌀 Never use a damaged wire.
- 🌀 Never put anything other than a plug into a wall socket.
- 🌀 Do not use electricity near water.

5.3 Making a circuit

The electricity from cells is less powerful than mains electricity. Small cells are safe to use. Touching the metal parts will not give you an electric shock.

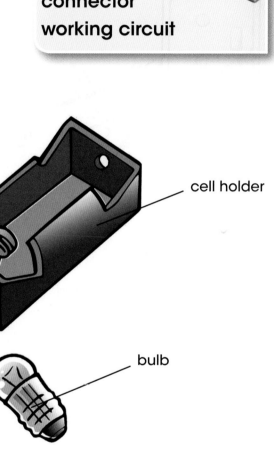

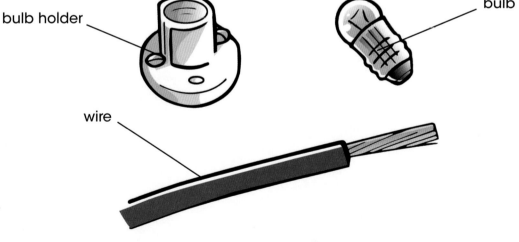

cell

cell holder

positive

negative

bulb holder

bulb

wire

A cell pushes electricity around a **circuit**. It has a positive (+) side and a negative (−) side. The **bulb** lights up when electricity goes through it. The wire is used as a **connector**.

Activity 5.3

You will need:

a cell · a cell holder
a bulb · a bulb holder
two or more wires

Can you make a bulb light up?

Try making a circuit. You will need to connect the cell to the bulb using wires. Does the bulb light up?

This **working circuit** makes a loop. Electricity comes out of the cell at the negative (−) end. It moves around the loop in the metal part of the wire then it goes back into the cell at the positive (+) end.

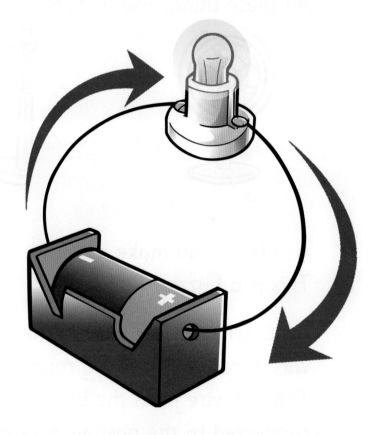

What you have learnt

🌀 A bulb, cell and wires can make a working circuit.

🌀 A bulb uses electricity to make light.

5.4 Using motors and buzzers

A **motor** can make things spin round. This is a motor.

All these things use motors.

 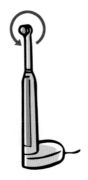 

A **buzzer** can make a sound. This is a buzzer.

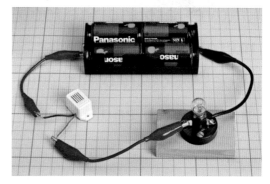

A buzzer will only work if the wires are the right way round. The red wire from the buzzer must be connected to the positive side of the cell.

All these things use buzzers.

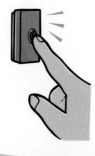  

Activity 5.4a

Making a fan

Modupe is making a fan using a motor and card. Make a fan like this.

Now make a circuit to make it spin.

Connect the cell to the motor with wires to make a loop. Which way does the fan spin?

Now change the wires over at the cell.

What do you think will happen?

Activity 5.4b

Using a buzzer

Make the buzzer work in a circuit.

Now change the wires over at the cell. What do you think will happen?

What you have learnt

- Motors use electricity to make things turn.
- Buzzers use electricity to make sound.

5.5 Switches

A **switch** can be used to turn electricity on or off.

What do you think these switches do?

Word to learn

switch

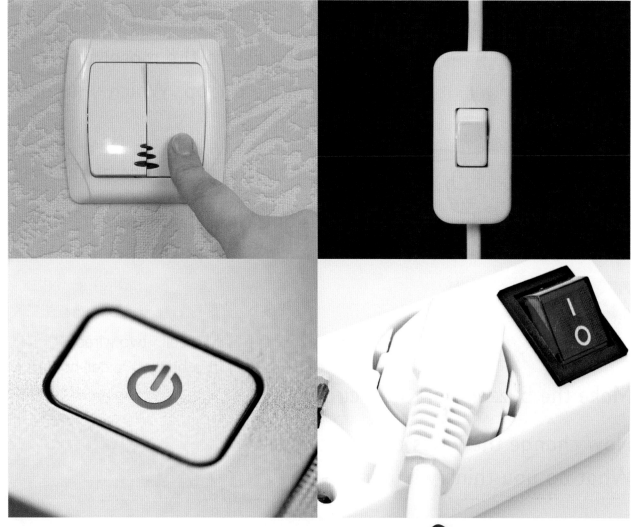

Safety Never touch a switch with wet hands.

Activity 5.5

Switch it on, switch it off

Use a switch to make a circuit like this.

You will need:

a bulb, motor or buzzer
a switch • a cell
three wires
a cell holder

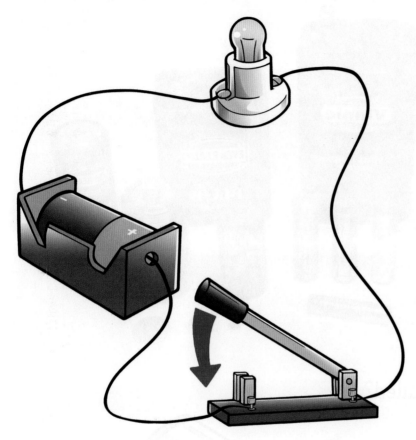

The switch makes a gap in the circuit.

The electricity cannot move around the loop.

Try changing the bulb for a buzzer or motor.

What do you think will happen?

What you have learnt

Electricity can be turned on and off using switches.

5.6 Check your progress

1 These have two names. What are they?

2 What are these called?

a

b

c

d

3 Will these circuits work?

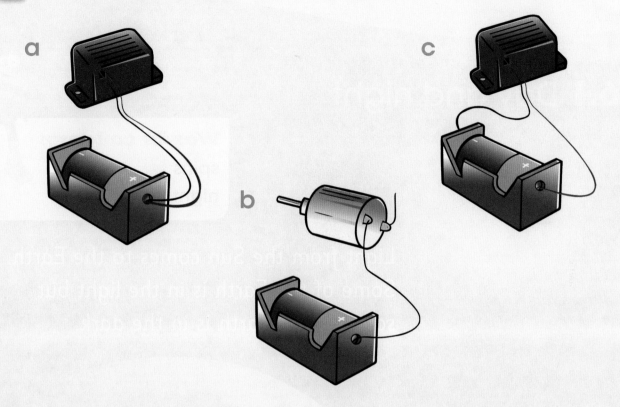

a

c

b

4 Will the bulb be on or off in these circuits? Why?

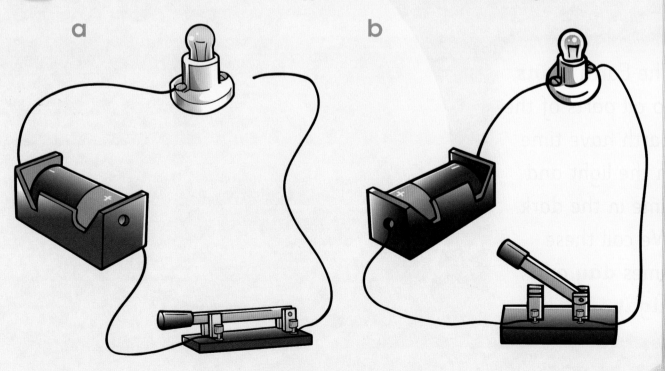

a

b

6 The Earth and the Sun

6.1 Day and night

Light from the Sun comes to the Earth. Some of the Earth is in the light but some of the Earth is in the dark.

The Earth **spins** so all parts of the Earth have time in the light and time in the dark. We call these times **day** and **night**.

Activity 6.1

Day and night

You will need:

a toy person
a globe or football
sticky tack
a light source

Imran and Ali are showing how we get day and night.

Try doing this.

Talk about when it is day or night for your toy person.

Look at this picture of the Earth.

Which part is day?

Which part is night?

What you have learnt

🌀 We get day and night because the Earth spins.

What do you think?

Activity 6.2

Does the Sun move?

Find the Sun in the sky but do not look straight at it.

Draw a picture to show where it is and write down the time.

Do this at different times in the day.

Safety Never look straight at the Sun. It can damage your eyes.

12.00 p.m.

10.00 a.m

2.00 p.m.

8.00 a.m.

4.00 p.m.

The Sun looks as though it moves across the sky because the Earth spins. Places move from night to day and from day to night. When you are standing on the Earth, it looks like the Sun is moving.

What you have learnt

🌀 The Earth spins and it looks like the Sun is moving.

6.3 Changing shadows

Activity 6.3a

Do shadows move?

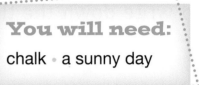

You will need:

chalk • a sunny day

Go outside at different times. Ask a friend to draw round your shadow. Stand in the same place each time or your test will be **unfair**.

What do you think will happen? Will your shadow be in the same place each time?

This is a sundial. Can you see the shadow?

As the Earth turns past the Sun, shadows move too.

On a sundial the shadow tells the time. Look at the picture. Can you tell what time it is?

Activity 6.3b

Shadow length

Rita is measuring the length of shadows.

Does the length of a shadow change?

She wants to answer a question.

Measure the length of a shadow at different times.

What do you think will happen?

In the morning and evening the Sun is low and shadows are long.

At midday the Sun is higher in the sky and shadows are shorter.

What you have learnt

- Shadows move slowly as the Earth spins.
- Shadows are short when the Sun is high.
- Shadows are long when the Sun is low.

1 Look at the picture.

Who is in day? Who is in night? Can you say why?

2 Which picture is right, A or B?

A

B

3 Look at these pictures.

A

B

a Is the Sun high or low in these pictures?
b Do you think it is morning, midday or evening?

Reference

How to look carefully and record what you find out

Think of a question

Tao and Dana have found some minibeasts.

Tao has a question.

Dana says what she thinks the answer is.

Talk about what to do

Tao and Dana are going to look at the minibeasts and make a tally chart.

Look carefully to find out

They look at each minibeast carefully.

Dana uses a magnifying glass. She moves the magnifying glass slowly until she can see clearly.

Record what you find out

Dana counts the legs. Tao adds the numbers to the tally chart.

Tao draws one line for each minibeast in the right place on the chart.

0 legs	2 legs	4 legs	6 legs	8 legs
||			|||/|||	||

Number of minibeasts		0 legs	2 legs	4 legs	6 legs	8 legs
	5				🦋	
	4				🦋	
	3				🦋	
	2	🦋			🦋	🦋
	1	🦋			🦋	🦋

After looking at all the minibeasts they make a block chart.

Some mini-beasts have no legs.

Talk about what you find out

Tao and Dana look at the block chart. They say what they have found out.

We found lots of minibeasts with six legs.

The Sun is very bright. Looking at it will damage your eyes.

Take care with other bright light sources. These can also damage your eyes.

Be careful with your ears too.

Loud sounds and loud music can damage your ears.

When you try to answer a science question, you must think about what could go wrong. You must think about how to avoid danger.

Arwa wants to know how materials change when heated.

But she is not being safe.

What dangers can you see?

What might happen?

How can Arwa stay safe?

Glossary and index

day	the time when a place on the Earth is facing the Sun – the hours of daylight	60
diamond	very hard, clear rock used in jewellery and for cutting hard objects	18
dissolve	when a solid becomes part of a liquid, for example salt dissolves in water	35
Earth	the planet we live on	16
elastic	a material that stretches easily and can go back to the shape it started as	30
electric shock	when electricity goes into your body – a big shock can hurt or kill you	50
electricity	we use it to make things like lights, computers and televisions work	48
extreme	very great or severe – for example, extreme cold means very, very cold	12
fair (test)	a test where you only change one thing and keep other things the same	35
forecasters	people who say what they think the weather will be like	12
frosty	very cold and icy	11
granite	very hard rock which comes from volcanoes, made of small pieces of different colours – we use it for building	16
hail	small bits of ice which fall like rain	11

heat	to make hotter	32
hot	a temperature which is high	33
ice	water that has become solid	33
light	bright glow from a light source that allows us to see things	38
limestone	grey rock which can contain fossils – we use it for building	16
liquid	a material that can flow or be poured – water is a liquid, for example	33
litter	unwanted materials that people have dropped, making a place untidy	8
mains electricity	powerful electricity we use in buildings	49
man-made	made by people – not found in nature	23
marble	hard, smooth, white rock – we use it for building and making statues and tiles	18
measure	to find the size or amount of something, for example length or time	7
melt	to change from a solid to a liquid	33
minibeasts	small animals like ants, spiders, ladybirds, butterflies, bees, flies	7
Moon	the large object that goes round the Earth and we see in the sky at night	39
motor	an object that uses electricity to make something move	54

natural	comes from nature – not man-made	22
night	the time when a place on the Earth is facing away from the Sun – the hours of darkness	60
predict	to say what you think will happen	35
protect	to look after something	8
quarry	a place where rocks are dug out of the ground	17
quartz	hard, shiny rock – clocks and radios use quartz	18
rain	water that falls in drops from clouds	10
record	to write, draw or photograph something that was seen or happened	7
reflect	if something reflects light, the light shines back from that object	39
research	to find out about something, for example by using books or the internet	13
rock	hard part of the Earth's surface	16
same	just like something else, not different	11
sand	loose brown material made from very small pieces of rock	21
sandy	covered with sand or made mostly of sand	21
sandstone	red, brown or orange rock made from sand that has become hard – we use it for building	16

sewage	waste water from your shower, bath, washing machine, dishwasher, kitchen sink and toilet	8
shadow	an area of darkness we see when an object blocks light	42
shape	the outline of an object, for example square, cube, curved	26
slate	hard rock, often blue, grey or purple, which breaks easily into flat thin pieces – we cut it to make roof tiles	18
snow	ice that falls in soft, white flakes	11
soil	the natural material on the surface of the Earth in which plants grow	20
solid	a material that keeps its shape and does not flow	33
spin	to turn round and round about a point	60
squash	to change the shape of an object by pushing or crushing it – making it shorter	26
stone	a small piece of rock	21
storm	weather with strong wind, a lot of cloud and rain, and sometimes thunder and lightning	13
stretch	change the shape of a material by pulling – making it longer or wider	26

Sun	the nearest star to Earth – it gives us heat and light	39
sunny	bright weather that happens when the Sun is shining	11
switch	something that can break the flow of electricity in a circuit	56
tally chart	a chart we use for counting things by drawing small lines	69
temperature	how hot or cold something is	10
torch	a small object you hold in your hand which uses a battery to make light	40
twist	change the shape of an object by turning parts of it in different ways	26
unfair (test)	a test where you change more than one thing	64
warm	a temperature which is not hot and not cold	11
weather	wind, sunshine, temperature, rain, snow and so on	10
wind	movement of air	10
wire	a piece of metal that electricity flows through – we use it to connect things together in a circuit	50
working circuit	a loop that electricity can flow around	53

Acknowledgements

The authors and publisher are grateful for the permissions granted to reproduce copyright materials. While every effort has been made, it has not always been possible to identify the sources of all the materials used, or to trace all the copyright holders. If any omissions are brought to our notice, we will be happy to include the appropriate acknowledgements on reprinting.

The publisher is grateful to the experienced teachers Mansoora Shoaib Shah, Lahore Grammar School, 55 Main, Gulberg, Lahore and Lynne Ransford for their careful reviewing of the content.

p. 7l Andrew Zarivny/ Shutterstock; p. 7r zroakez/ Shutterstock; p. 9 Jim West/ Alamy; p. 11 scott masterton/Flickr/ Getty Images; p. 13 World History Archive/Image Asset Management Ltd./ Alamy; p. 16tl Guenter Fischer/imagebroker/ Alamy; p. 16tr Don Paulson Photography/Purestock/ RGB Ventures LLC dba SuperStock/ Alamy; p. 16bl Andrey Lebedev/ Shutterstock; p. 16br Valery Shanin/ Shutterstock; p. 17t Core/ Shutterstock; p. 17b Alessandro Colle/ Shutterstock; p. 18tl E.R. Degginger/ Alamy; p. 18tr Natural History Museum, London/ Science Photo Library; p. 18cl Charles D. Winters/ Science Photo Library; p. 18br Doug Martin/ Science Photo Library; p. 18bl Susan E. Degginger/ Alamy; p. 27l ASP/YPP/INSADCO Photography/ Alamy; p. 27r Michael Flippo/ Alamy; p. 28cl Evgeny Murtola/ Shutterstock; p. 28cr Zoonar/Lebedev Valeriy/Zoonar GmbH / Alamy; p. 28bl dbtravel/dbimages/ Alamy; p. 28br Valerie Garner/ Alamy; p. 30t elina/ Shutterstock; p. 30b OlegD/ Shutterstock; p. 31 David Eulitt/Kansas City Star/MCT via Getty Images/ Getty Images; p. 33 Pavel Isupov/ Shutterstock; p. 34 Thomas Schneider/imagebroker / Alamy; p. 39tl D and D Photo Sudbury/ Shutterstock; p. 39tcl dlnicolas/ Shutterstock; p. 39tcr Timur Kulgarin/ Shutterstock; p. 39tr Iconica/PM Images/ Getty Images; p. 40 Grant Dixon/Lonely Planet Images/ Getty Images; p. 42 Ocean/ Corbis; p. 44 Credinet/Imagehit Inc./ Alamy; p. 49tr Oleg Zaslavsky/ Shutterstock; p. 49bl revers/ Shutterstock; p. 49br sciencephotos/ Alamy; p. 50 demarcomedia/ Shutterstock; p. 54t David J. Green – engineering themes / Alamy; p. 54b Martyn F. Chillmaid/ Science Photo Library; p. 56tl Boris Sosnovyy/ Shutterstock; p. 56tr Westergren/ iStockphoto; p. 56bl Kostenko Maxim/ Shutterstock; p. 56br FuzzBones/ Shutterstock; p. 58 sciencephotos/ Alamy; p. 61 NASA/NOAA/ Science Photo Library; p. 65 CRM/ Shutterstock

Cover artwork: Bill Bolton

l = left, r = right, t = top, b = bottom, c = centre